TELLING THE TIME

Carol Watson
Illustrated by David Higham
Consultant: Wyn Brooks

Deputy-Head Teacher of The Coombes School, Arborfield, Berkshire; lectures widely on Primary School Mathematics.

50p

With thanks to Joseph and Chloe Sl

D0674019

It is night-time. A spaceship lands on the earth.

Out of the spaceship steps a robot.
He is called DG1.

The sun rises. It is morning. DG1 decides to explore.

He meets Professor Blink, the clockmaker, on his morning walk.

3

"Who are you?" asks the Professor.

"I am DG1. I am a Digital Time Teller.
Look, I have the time written on my front."

"I use my pocketwatch to tell the time,"
says the Professor.

"What a strange thing," says DG1.
"How can you tell the time with that?"

"Come into my workshop and see," answers Professor Blink.

The workshop is full of different clocks.

"A clock has a face," says the Professor. "The numbers 1 to 12 are written round the edge."

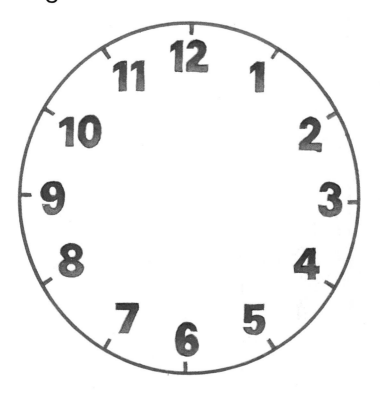

"These are for counting the hours. Find 1, then read the numbers round the clock."

"A clockface has two pointers. One is short and the other is longer."

"They are called the little hand and the big hand."

8

"The big hand moves very slowly pointing to the minute marks round the edge of the clock."

"In this picture, there are minute numbers as well as marks. Most clocks only have the marks but no numbers."

"The little hand moves even more slowly and points to the numbers on the clock face."

"We read the hour by looking at the number nearest to the little hand."

"This clock says 8 o'clock. The little hand points to 8 and the big hand points to 12." says the Professor.

"What is o'clock?" asks DG1.

"O'clock means it is exactly on the hour," says the Professor. When it is o'clock the big hand always points to 12 and the little hand points to the number of the hour."

1 o'clock

"Can you see what time it is on all these clocks?"

At 12 o'clock it is lunchtime.
Professor Blink cuts up a pie. He cuts it
in half, then into quarters.

"You can divide up a clockface just like
this pie," he says.

"When the big hand has moved a quarter of the way round the clock it is quarter past the hour."

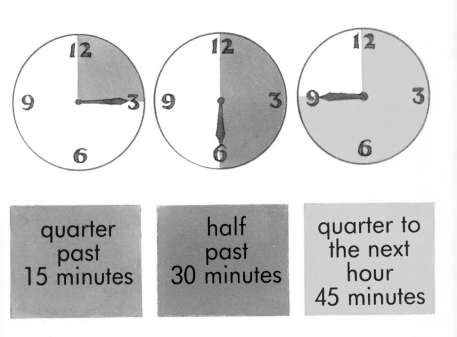

| quarter past 15 minutes | half past 30 minutes | quarter to the next hour 45 minutes |

"Halfway round is half past and three quarters of the way round is quarter to the next hour."

"Tell me more about these minute marks around the edge," says DG1

"Each mark stands for 1 minute. There are 60 minutes in one hour. Can you count up to 60?"

"My digital clock counts for me,"
says DG1.

"The time is 12.25," says the Professor.
"The big hand has moved round
25 minutes. We can call it 25 minutes past
12 o'clock."

"Try to remember that there are 5 minutes between each of the numbers on the clock."

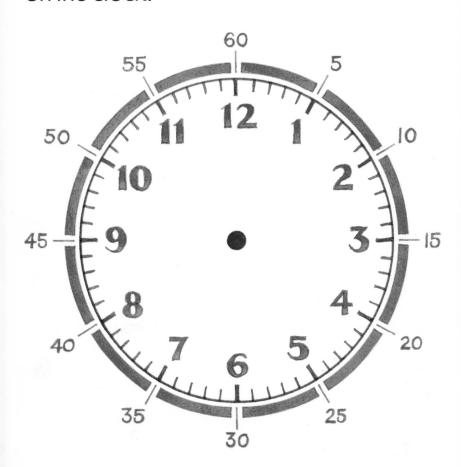

"Do you know how many minutes of the hour have gone by on these clocks?"

Professor Blink and DG1 talk for a long time. At 7 o'clock they have supper.

It gets later and later. The Professor feels tired.

"My goodness, it's midnight", says the Professor. "We must go to bed." "What is midnight?" asks DG1.

12 O'CLOCK CHART

"When both the big hand and the little hand point to 12, it is 12 o'clock. At night-time it is called midnight. In the daytime it is called midday or noon."

Next day the Professor and DG1 wake up very late. "Good morning," says DG1. "It's nearly 12 o'clock," says Professor Blink. "It will soon be midday."

"Did you know that the time before midday is morning and the time after it is afternoon?"

"We have a code for that," says DG1.
"The time before midday is called a.m.
and the time after it is called p.m."

"We use that code too," replies the
Professor.

DG1 stays with the Professor for a while.
They spend a lot of time together.

Can you tell which of these pictures are a.m. and which are p.m.?

At last it is time for DG1 to go home.
His spaceship is waiting. The
Professor gives him a clock as a
present and they wave each other
goodbye.

First published in 1984
Usborne Publishing Ltd
20 Garrick St, London
WC2 9BJ, England
© Usborne Publishing Ltd 1984

The name of Usborne and the
device 🎈 are Trade Marks of
Usborne Publishing Ltd.
Printed in Portugal